"*Book of Expression* is more that a mere poetry book; it's a form of personal therapy for the author and reader alike. Each page jolts the psyche from the darkness with its sheer beauty, vulnerability, and emotion."

—**Eva Xan, Poetry Book Editor** & *Author of Esoterra*

INTOXICATING EXPRESSIONS

Terrell L. Cuffee

INTRODUCTION

In the realm of poetry, there exists a profound power to capture the essence of our lives, our emotions, and the world around us. It is within these lines, these verses, that we find solace, reflection, and the opportunity to share our innermost thoughts with others. In the pages that follow, I invite you to delve into the intoxicating expressions that have emerged from the depths of my soul.

Inspiration, that elusive spark that fuels our creativity, manifests itself in myriad forms. For me, it is unequivocally embodied in the radiant souls that call me "Dad." My children, three beautiful beings who have graced my life, have become the very source of my transformation. Since their arrival, my existence has been forever altered, and with each passing day, I am reminded of the profound responsibility I bear—to pave a better life for them, to provide unwavering stability, and to be a living testament of the best version of myself. They have become my guiding light, my teachers in the delicate art of fatherhood, and the catalysts for my own growth and evolution. It is through their eyes that I have come to understand the depths of unconditional love, and it is their laughter that ignites the fire within my creative spirit.

Yet, my muse extends beyond the boundaries of my immediate experience. I draw upon the rich tapestry of personal encounters, observing the lives and trials of others around me. Their stories intertwine with my own, weaving a narrative that reflects the universal human experience. It is through the lens of these shared moments that my emotions, thoughts, and actions find their voice in written expression.

In the pursuit of authenticity, I am inspired by those who dare to be different, who break free from the confines of societal norms, and who defy expectations. They are the individuals who transform nothingness into something extraordinary, who fight tirelessly for their dreams, and who fearlessly dismantle the barriers and boundaries that stand in their way. Their unwavering resolve and indomitable spirit have become a source of inspiration, urging me to push the limits of my creativity and explore uncharted territories within my own artistry.

"Intoxicating Expressions" is an embodiment of these influences. It is a journey through the intricacies of life, a testament to the transformative power of parenthood, and a celebration of the human spirit's resilience. Within these pages, you will find a collection of poems that explore the full spectrum of emotions, navigating the depths of joy, pain, love, and longing.

In this collection, "Intoxicating Expressions," you will bear witness to the culmination of these inspirations. It is a symphony of words that dances across the page, inviting you to explore the boundless depths of human emotion and connection. Through writing, I have found solace and sanctuary, a form of personal therapy that allows me to make sense of the world and my place within it.

May these intoxicating expressions resonate with your own experiences, stir your heart, and transport you to a realm where words dance with raw vulnerability and unbridled passion. Join me as we embark on this poetic odyssey, where the boundaries of imagination cease to exist, and the power of words knows no bounds.

ACKNOWLEDGMENTS

Thanks to:

Editor- "Eva Xan", Poetry Book Editor & *Author of Esoterra for her fantastic Editorial services*

Book Cover- anaz@strongdayart ig strongday_art

Interior Layout- JBookDesigns on Fiverr

DEDICATION

This book is dedicated to the resilient souls who have traversed the depths of darkness, to those who have endured traumatic experiences both firsthand and through the lens of empathy. It is for those who bear the weight of fear and vulnerability, stemming from violence and the harrowing grasp of mental and emotional abuse. To the uneducated and the voiceless, this dedication is a tribute to your strength.

Within these pages, I extend my hand to the mentally and emotionally unstable, offering solace and understanding. This work is for those who have suffered the irreparable loss of someone close and dear, for those who carry the weight of heartbreak in their souls.

To those suffocated by the culture of problematic drug and alcohol use, I offer compassion and hope. May these words provide a lifeline to those yearning to break free from the chains that bind them.

For those who face the daily onslaught of racism and bias, this dedication is a testament to your resilience and a reminder that you are not alone. May these writings serve as a source of empowerment, a catalyst for change, and a beacon of hope in the face of adversity.

To those who long to escape the confines of societal norms, I embrace you. May these words grant you the freedom to explore the vast depths of your true self, unfettered by judgment and expectations.

Finally, I extend my deepest gratitude to all who have embraced me for who I am and respected my journey. Your unwavering support and acceptance have fortified my spirit and fueled my creative endeavors. It is for you, dear reader, that these writings were born.

May this book offer solace, inspiration, and a sense of belonging to all who seek refuge within its pages. May it serve as a gentle reminder that, despite the hardships we endure, there is light to be found amidst the shadows, and hope to be discovered in even the darkest corners of our lives.

With heartfelt gratitude,
Terrell L. Cuffee

CONTENTS

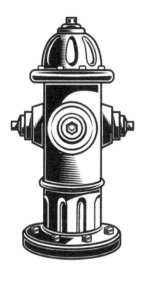

SECTION 1
BEREAVEMENT

GONE INTO THE LIGHT

The phone rang slower than ever.
The rings were far apart and lingered.
The house shook as the last ring
was destined to be answered.
A familiar voice said my name.
I drug my tone across the phone line:
"What's up?"

The voice replied,
"Your father had a heart attack.
We're at the Hospital."
I grabbed the first pair of clothing in sight and proceeded.
The night passed by the car window slowly
with all the possible outcomes painted in sight.

My arrival was greeted with hugs and kisses.
Family members had preceded me.
I was told to go in a small room where we waited.
A lot of questions were yet to be answered.
A man with a white jacket came in and began to speak.
He spoke, and spoke, and spoke, yet said nothing.

My emotions rose,
and that's when I knew:
My father was no more.
From the tip of my toes to the pit of my throat,
that's when I knew:
My father had gone into the light.

DUE TO MY DEMISE

I stepped into a room full of moping and crying. I looked face to face to get a little more detail. The room was filled with clouds as if a thunderstorm was enduring. Discussions developed pertaining to life insurance and funeral arrangements. My wife, mother, grandmother, aunts, and mother-in-law were all present. This was all for me.

They talked about the good times we had together as smiles filled the room. This rush of energy was followed by an echo of silence, then a burst of sadness. My mother rushed out of the room heavily weeping. I tried to comfort them all by touching without being felt and talking without being heard. I thought my voice was loud and clear as I spoke directly in everyone's ear, but no one responded. I kept reiterating that I was alright.

A brave soul whispered the words: Did you hear him? They responded one by one: I heard him too. I connected to everyone in spirit. My soul was present, but to the eyes, I was lost. My feelings gleefully rang as I spoke my last words they would ever hear: I'm alright. Everything is going to be alright. My heart sped up as I descended with a sweaty awakening, sitting up in my bed, feeling my body and thanking God. I also thought about how much love I have to give, how much caring I have left to do.

I have just seen the distress of my passing...

MY LOST FRIENDS

Every day, I heard knocks on my door,
and I'd know it was you, balls bouncing.
We laughed and joked due to our mutual comfort.
I looked for you, and every day, you looked for me.

There was not a day when we didn't see eye to eye.
We walked by and competed just to compete.
When was it that you didn't challenge me,
to test the heap, to defeat the odds?

All the days I knew you, I knew you most.
We were different, but that made us complete.
Together like a train and tracks, we made sense—
anytime without you, minus one of the clique.

Most days, it was about six to eight of us
or eight to twelve of us: some clean, some dirty.
We stayed out of trouble and wanted to have fun.
We found trouble but just wanted to have fun.

Nowadays, I don't see you, and you don't see me.
Most days, I'm alone, stronger than ever on my way.
I remember all of you and will never stop loving you.
We all had peanut heads, hats never too big.

When I see you, it's strange and awkward like
two strangers forced to engage in conversation
with no common goal. How did this happen?
When your birthdays pop up, I still call.

When it's mine, I know you will return the favor.
What's wrong with a call every so often?
I look to the sky every so often, searching.
Every day, I miss you like my brothers were lost.

Not a day goes by when I don't remember that we grew together.
Not a day goes by when I don't realize we grew apart.
The place you have in my heart will never fade, but sometimes,
I feel like the sight when the eyelids close: my friends are gone.

SHORTEST FRIENDSHIP

I met you while watching basketball and we talked.
You were so consciously aware of life and its obstacles.
I would have never thought you were homeless.
We exchanged advice about our business ventures.
Your face became very familiar at work,
but strangely, I didn't see you for a while...

My boss talked about a man who died
in one of the school bathrooms, and I listened.
Days went by, and a security officer stopped me
to ask if I had heard about my buddy. I said no.
The description he gave me was the same that my boss
spoke of. I didn't know it was you. It hurt as if I knew
you for life. What's sad is I didn't get to say goodbye...

SURE DEATH

One foot plants at nine o'clock, the other at three,
rooting on the boards that collect to form a pier.
This path to earth's most abundant element forms a plank.
Eyes gaze a distance beyond the horizon where there lies:
Life,   Hope,   & Promise.

The weather changes, providing an initial warning.
Wind takes everything light,
while Ocean lifts up and dives back into itself.
Water is rising over sea-level inch by inch,
elevating until boards are blurred by sandy sea.

Feet and ankles descend beneath salty waters.
Knees and thighs follow urging hips and torso to make way.
Yet, the heart ponders; therefore, the body remains.
The water level is chin-high, causing the head to tilt,
securing   precious   air.

Respect for respiratory passageways peaks.
A gasp that endures, flashbacks of wariness.
Sure death that could have been avoided lingers.
At a standstill, pictures of what could have been are
engulfed   by   what is.

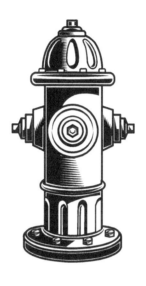

SECTION 2

LOVE AND HEARTACHE

REUNITING LOVE

I smile as she walks toward me.
The glow covets her bodily fortress
like a portrait of light surrounded
by nature's frame.

My grin only hides the irrepressible
outburst of happiness built inside.
I want to look as if I am in control;
I will continue to stay cool.

Her progress only makes me weak.
This magnificence draws near.
The light descends, showing her emotions.
Her eyes slant, her cheeks rise, her teeth gleam.

My body is motionless.
The only thing with movement is the bead
of sweat drawing a sideburn on my face,
positioning under my chin, hanging on.

She stops in front of me and raises her arm,
reaching for the worry and securing it
in the palm of her hand.
She then clutches it
and pulls it to her heart.

Her hands touch my face with elegance.
Her lips slowly meet mine.
We perfectly complete what was missing:
reuniting love.

GUILTY CONSCIENCE

What have I done? Everything is becoming bleak.
The air is getting thin, and the walls are closing in.
It feels like the last kick to get to the top of the ocean.
Fingers touch the surface hoping to capture that last
grasp of life. My body feels surrounded by multitudes
of water, salted like meat in hope of preservation—
only I'm getting dissolved, passing into the solution.

There has to be a solution! The days are growing long,
but the hours are becoming short. Time is not on my side.
This is the making of an old man: gray hairs, wrinkling skin,
aching back, tired days, worry-filled nights, hiding, ducking,
trying not to get caught, yet my capture is approaching—
lingering like a vulture ready to devour my flesh.

Because of carelessness, I can play no more.
I'm jammed in a double life where the odds are stacked
against me: two women, two different directions... too much.
Now I'm caught up with strong feelings for both beauties
while fighting my own internal demons: right and left hooks
that I self-impose due to my hunger for the opposite sex,
baiting me in for closure during soaring emotions
and calling out the wrong name.

I'm getting caught up in my own twist, I'm getting tired
of erasing numbers from my cell, possessing excessive
e-mail addresses, driving to the next town to catch a movie,
and running from the truth. It's time to take it easy
and plan my life accordingly: one woman, maybe a house,
a picket fence with a dog, marriage, and a couple of kids...
Yet, I am afraid of commitment, afraid to trust;
afraid to get hurt, afraid to make a wrong choice;
afraid to be made a fool, afraid to face karma.

THE OTHER SIDE

Sometimes, love can be wrong:
bad timing, two-faced
filled with deception—

an unruly desire that
can only be controlled by
acceptance or denial.

Sometimes, love turns into hate
filled with sinister thoughts.
Love is an emotion that can switch sides.

THIS EMOTION

This emotion is a troublemaker. It always gets me off track. I can't focus on things that really matter anymore when this emotion takes place. Sometimes, I can avoid this emotion, depending on the circumstances. All the extra incentives that make this emotion not worthwhile helps me to keep away from it. Sometimes, this emotion just sneaks up on me and kicks me in the ass. When that happens, I lose my cool. Everyone around that knows my state of presence recognizes when I am trapped in this emotion.

Sometimes, this emotion takes time to develop. When this happens, I am better prepared to deal with it. I look for this emotion because I have been without it for such a long time. I feel down when I can't find it. It always must be at arm's reach, even when I am not in search of it.

Sometimes, this emotion happens too fast, and it creates a problem because it's all I have. This emotion can wake you up in the middle of the night. Other times, it just makes you want to throw things around. This emotion can turn into hate. Most of the time, this emotion causes a lot of distrust. It can also set the mood for other activities.

This emotion requires a lot of time. It is not just an emotion you can put in your pocket and pull out when you have time for it. This emotion can make you lose valuable sleep. This emotion can make your hobbies become non-existent. This emotion can cause headaches. This emotion can take over your entire world. This emotion can cause bad decisions. This emotion must be controlled. When this emotion is shared, it can be a wonderful feeling. This emotion is a beautiful thing. This emotion helps create beautiful babies: LOVE.

YELLOW!

The sight of her name appearing
on my caller ID brought a smile to my face.
I let it ring once more to prepare to answer:
Yellow!

She started talking, but the noise
in my background was smothering.
I had to get somewhere quiet,
somewhere with four closed walls—
just me and my phone:
Yellow!

She said hey, and my gut contracted.
Her voice, her conversation, her intelligence
her experience, her sense of humor,
and her magnetic energy all had me feeling vulnerable.
Suddenly, things went silent. I spoke:
Yellow!

She said she got my message,
but her phone was acting up.
I didn't believe her, but I didn't care.
All that mattered was now.
Now I was jittery, listening to every word precisely.
I told her I wanted to see her.
She asked, "When?"
I replied, "Soon."
There was silence again:
Yellow!

She responded with a sexy "it's cool".
My heart sped up; I told her I would call her back.
She said okay, and I began to speak again
to tell her when I would call her.
I got no response.
Yellow!
Yellow!
Yellow!

BOOK OF LITTLE RESISTANCE

The book lay awaiting my approach.
Opening its hard cover as if there was a breeze,
the pages blew to its destined passage.
I drew closer and closer while batting my eyes.
Gaining focus, I witnessed words as they cleared.

The letters presented a seductive aroma,
justifying my reach; therefore, I obeyed.
My hands shook gently, which was only noticeable to me.
My fingers touched first, my pointer, then my ring,
and I split its meaning with my index.

Caressing the letters of its words—
back and forth, round and round, up and down—
I studied them, showing my admiration and desire to fulfill.
The cover closed on my hand and drew in a further touch,
convincing me to blow out the candles.

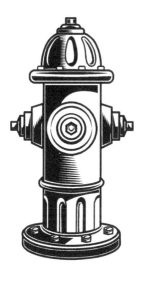

SECTION 3
INTROSPECTION

STORM CLOUD

A cloud hovers over like a mercy demon,
covering the earth's surface
while moving through the air
like smoke from a chimney,
only horizontally.

It stops, it sits, and it pours,
leaving crystal tears that part the air—
obeying gravity,
attacking the ground like tires on vehicles,
giving it a heartbeat faster than no other,
and leaving its mark.

A shaded ground reflects its mirrored self—
an exchange of elements that will one day
mist back to the demon's eye.
It has overstayed its welcome
and nomadically seeks another sequel of steps,
scattering hydro upon dehydrated land,
filling cracks in concrete,
and giving the temporary wholeness.

WORKING IN MY DREAMS

I rise from my fetal position, gasping for air.
My heart feels like it has invaded the area between
my flesh and the skin that covers my chest.
It beats thunderously, echoing in my throat.

I reach for my face in hope of feeling my life,
touching deftness disguised as beads of sweat.

I wake up feeling like I was never asleep,
placing the drama from my dream in order
piece by piece in search of a clue as to why
I work all day, then persist to fight all night.

INNOCENTFUL

Without guilt like
a prowl unheard, unnoticed,
where daybreak sneaks up
like an idea first turned
away, then excepted gracefully.

The face of delightfulness
tiptoes with precise elegance.
Movement just as movements,
yet silent like a ballerina's bow.

To be innocentful is to be as far
from disruption or disturbance
as possible, to walk with a
craftiness polished by sheer motion
under the watchful eye of others—

a peaceful approach like that
of a child asking your name,
then carrying on the most untainted
conversation one could ever
imagine...

SHE RUNS FROM HER SHADOW

Her shadow follows her.
She can't escape her dark self.
It lingers around like a murky demon,
posing still when she stops;
running when she runs and keeping up.

Her only safety is at night
or under a shaded tree when sunny.
She avoids looking back, for it is
there waiting for her next move,
mocking her without showing face.

She walks backwards
to avoid seeing her banshee
Afraid to face her gloomy persona,
she asks a question to the sun:
How can something so beautiful
create such a phantom?

She stays away from the day,
for she knows it's a trick.
Everything created by this life-giving form
of energy has a birthmark,
and it shows up in the day, waiting to haunt.
Now she's working on how to face dawn...

BESTOWING OPTIMISM

Escape with the mind,
and the body will follow like
a kite in autumn catching the breeze.
You only have yourself to count on
and God to guide your actions.

You are a strong reflection of your culture.
Things look bleak now, but for every
dark day, expect a sky that's blue.
Raise your arms towards heaven.
End this curfew of mental blockage.

Allow yourself to reconnect with your past.
Flash back through the mind like
a pointed remote remembering
impossibilities and deterred attempts
that show you how you overcame
being cemented by rumbling grounds.

Close your eyes and reawaken.
What's awake must be sound.
Look around; no one is near.
The air is clear like the echo of silence
yet frustrating like walls with no escape.

Absorb, then regurgitate.
Understand that feeling;
Others are going through it too.
Give back what has made you
complete and administer the healing.
Look around; no one's near.
All around, your presence is here.

CRYING SKY

The clouds race across the sky
like stampedes of buffalo racing across the plains.
The birds circle, seemingly aware of what's to come.
Light clouds follow dark ones; dark clouds follow light ones.
Some are blended to perfection—
grayed like areas of uncertainty yet keeping pace.

The birds disappear into them,
gaining coverage as the sky starts to cry,
releasing an outburst of emotion.
Flashes of past, present, and future provide light.
Silence fills the air as the clouds part ways.
Light shines through the cracks.

The birds reappear and circle,
seemingly aware of what will pass.
The clouds race to their next destination,
directed by the elements of change.

GUT CHECK!

Everyone in Life has a journey.
That Journey through Life is what
I am most touched, driven, and inspired by.
All stories are different yet have similarities.
All journeys are made with emotion,
so I write through my emotions which are
reflected and caused by my life's experience.
The way I interpret them is my creative outcry.
The way I present them is my personal therapy.

These experiences are not all personal,
yet a lot are. Society's reflections inspire me
just as much as my interpersonal ones do.
Dreams are another trigger to creative aspirations.
Therefore, I embrace them. Dramatic occurrences
hold a place in my mind due to the level of emotion
caused by them, so my expression is drama.
I believe the truth is in your gut,
thus my writing is what I consider a

GUT CHECK!

HEAVY LEGS

The legs are heavy.
They cross for comfort,
one resting weight on the other.

If the legs go, the body will
follow like footprints in mud.
Life is a stride; light is ahead.

They can't take a step forward.
They're trapped by the force of gravity
and grounded by excess weight.

The arms are related by blood,
lending helping hands,
dragging and lifting the legs—

patting them on their thighs,
encouraging them to progress,
putting sneakers on and tying the laces.

INTO THE NIGHT

It's as if he could hear my thoughts.
I cringed as my troubles showed face.
I noticed him looking back several times;
He knew something was disturbing me.

From the back seat of the vehicle,
I asked the driver to turn up the music.
I wanted to drown any possibility of questions:
Are you alright? Want to talk about it?

My face pressed against the glass,
smudging its clear interior.
I felt lonely and the saturated pressures of life.
I knew no one would understand my pain.

My eyes were intricately open,
watching the street lights as they shone.
Each light tried to grab hold of me,
only to let go as distance cut off contact.

My mind raced through scenarios:
could haves, should haves—
only to accept what was.
He turned down the music and said in a foreign voice:

Follow the stars!
They will provide your light until the sun returns.
He turned around and turned the music back up.
My face lifted off the glass and I stared at him.

He stared into the night!

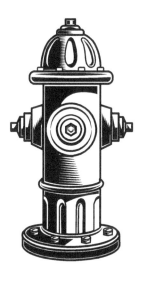

SECTION 4
ENDURING RACISM

DIALECT

Throughout my life,
I've had to adapt.
My words aren't precise,
yet my peers understand
me perfectly.

I've defended myself like
someone accused, waiving
away his rights to an attorney.

When I talk around you,
I feel uncomfortable,
claustrophobic, muzzled like
my words might cause
an outbreak of rabies.

Maybe I'm trying too hard
to help you understand.
When you try to talk like me,
I feel it's out of sarcasm.
You're overly belligerent
that your language is correct,
and mine is a result
of poor schooling.

I don't understand you either!
So, does that make you stupid?
I communicate perfectly
with my friends and family.
Isn't that what counts?
I respect your world,
I love mine,
and I could care less about
changing mine to fit yours.

I fear interviews because
I'm not allowed to be me.
I'm different. Can't you see?
That doesn't mean I can't get the job done,
and I'm definitely not going to rob you.
I know, I know:
Excuses, Excuses...
Look! I'm not changing
the way I talk.

LAY DOWN

I sat down as if I weren't involved.
A little shouting, some gestures...
I was just expressing my emotions.
That's all.

They pulled me off the train,
slamming me to the platform.
Codes and reception noise blurted on their radios.
I saw black boots walking and standing all around me.
They then began inching towards my face and head.
I closed my eyes.
There was no way to cover up, my hands behind my back, cuffed.
My attempt to move my face side to side was met with boot to cheek.

The scenery faded, then I began to wake, lifted by the chains.
Once directed out of the underground, flashing lights blurred my vision,
but a Samaritan noticed my discombobulating presence.
She responded, "Damn!"

When shoved into the patty wagon, the officers told me to "Lay down."
I didn't respond, so he grabbed his club and reiterated, "Lay Down."
So, I lied down.

IN MEMORY OF EMMETT TILL

In an attempt to seek opportunity,
a move for so many so often,
sparked the interest of Mrs. Till.
She embraced reflections of migration
from bottom to top, anticipating change.

An industry in need of workers
to add heed to revolution—
never mind what they were dragged here for.
They only grasp what the need is now.

Opportunity unforeseen became omnipresent.
Mrs. Till was proud.
Her offspring had contingency,
and this cumulative movement
instigated cultural assortments.

What became normal up top,
was not customary back bottom.
Naïve yet affirmative Emmett set his sights
back to the bottom.

Beneath all chance laid a cold truth:
The blood begotten arrived from reason.
The unknown was forsaken there,
but portraits hold the moments still,
with proof beyond reason of mixed coexistence.

His gutsy actions for the cause of tongue
resulted in reactions remembering the cannots.
Come with us, at first, abduction indeed...
No return, no unmistaken words, no restoration.

The source soon reverted to the bottom for justice,
for the world to see
the treatment of her root then, now her seed.
Eye's opened and doors closed but unlocked
a mutilation broadcasted.

For the country to acknowledge
the ways of its litter.
Pain and suffering out in the open!
Now there's concern...

A VIOLENT CULTURE

I know catz that will body your moms
and come to the funeral with flowers in arms,
singin' ya favorite song, actin' like King Kong.

The moon and stars are just a warning to y'all.
Lock all doors 'cause bodies droppin' like waterfalls.
Sweat pours without playin' ball 'cause you runnin'
from your corner stores, duckin' from the ruckus.

The nightfall ain't for all, only a select few.
Don't let ya man run ahead, packin' a tech or two.
The closest back be the back that's through.
Trigger fingers bust guns like they're brand new.

In the night, they get intimate yet insignificant.
You have to stay aware like you doin' a bid
and camouflage by buildings getting nice,
blowing thick smoke, an urban fog of essence.

They think soft thoughts blind the six senses,
so bullet shells hit the ground and bounce up
with repetition like a thunderous game of life.

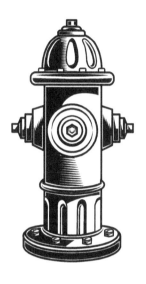

SECTION 5

GROWING UP
AND AGING

COMPLEX

Beneath my peers, I search for answers to my inability to develop. These shoes help out because I'm one of the shorter guys in my school. Everyone else sprouted over the summer, yet I was left behind. Homie had a pair that made him taller. I always had him by at least three inches. I'm wearing them so everyone will say "You got tall over the summer." I'm tired of just being cute; I want to be lofty.

There's some music artist that wears high heels, but they can do that. I don't think they care much about someone saying they look feminine. Besides, some like to wear pants with the ass portion cut out. I don't think high heels are going to affect them in any way. Me? I gotta keep it gutter; I'm from the hood. I can imagine how many noses I would have to break if someone says I look like a disco dancer in these.

I'm used to wearing Tim's. My clothes go nicely with them. Oh, here comes my beauty. I wonder if she's going to notice. I like this shorty; she's a dime piece. Hope she'll like the new me. If she does, I can never go back to being short again. I just hope the comedians and the rest of the flying lotus don't see me. They're my boys, but I have a task at hand, and they're not who I want to bump heads with. They notice everything.

I don't care; I'm in a different mind-state. I'll just put the mean face on like a prize fighter going for the title. They don't joke as much when I put the grill on. Anyway, I'm feeling these kicks: black, stylish, fat heels. I can get used to this look.

Damn, here this cat come, and he's looking down at my shoes. He better not say nothing. I'm going to whip his ass if he does. My beauty is standing here, and I refuse to be embarrassed in front of her.

HAIRSOME

A   little
mix of   Native
American,   African, and
European. My   hair grew long,
thick, and golden   brown   styled many ways:
corn rolls, box braids,   twist, Afros, and when it
rebelled, I called it wild man.   For the final   touch and a precise edge, I
went to Frankie, the master weaver.   He made your head look like an
artist sculptured every angle at ninety   degrees. Even gave sideburns to those
without. The combination was deadly: my hair and his tools. Many envied
me. *Grab your girls homeboy, my hair is done.* I was the executioner. Those
girls dropped dead when they got a load of me. *"Heyyy!"* They all said when
I coasted down the block, chin pointing straight forward in lead of the rest
of my gift. *I got this, ladies.* I know you saw me cut through the wind glowing
like precious jewels, stepping over the cracks in the cement without a look
beneath me—a flawless motion that put perfection to shame. Who would
have thought that a couple of years later, I would be told: *"Son, you losing
your hair."* All hell broke loose! Denial set in, my thickness grew thin, and
my forehead began to enlarge. I tried to hold on like a rubber band in a
ponytail. I tried vitamin E with aloe, Super Grow, African oil treatment,
and Indigenous herbs... Not even the master weaver's touch could save it, *rest
his soul.* I went into shock, stressed myself out, sped up the process, and let
it go. There was a fire, and my hair used the emergency exit. My chin grew
closer to my chest so I could feel every swallow of pride. I couldn't believe
how much I was complimented: *You look good with a bald head, more mature.*
My chin lifted up and led me through the mood, the air grazing my skull
with a liberal pat. Now, the shower dances on my clean bean without being
caught. I am alive again and adapted this new look, yet I'm humbler. I never
know when I'll have to modify it once more. When I cut it, the sun gets to
see how beautiful she is. When I let it grow, it looks like this poem, and I
can't wait to see the gray in it.

SUN AND THE SON

His dad called out to him, and he unpleasantly grabbed the basketball and began to straggle toward his father's car. His motion was one of disappointment. He wasn't ready to leave. He had not acquired his number of shots yet. Dad began to honk the horn in frustration. He wasn't moving fast enough, and instead continued to drop the ball, shoot, and fumble, which angered his dad more and more.

The temperature had dropped, but he continued to disobey his father because the adrenalin had taken control. His competitive fire gave him an edge in life. He looked around and saw that dad was in the car and not in the best mood. So, he began heading toward the car and stepped in front of the sun, leaning in a saddened way only to eclipse its rays. The sight was amazing. They merged and displayed one beautiful picture: his shape and form blending into the sunset, making the sun and the son one. He was giving life to this young person whose existence temporarily showcased the sun having his back. The most powerful star in the universe comforted dad, and all was good.

KADARI

The name means gods gift
When you came it was
You could be nothing else.
This description was yours
And yours only, a great king.

I remember waiting
Impatiently for your arrival
You were more impatient than I
Awaiting your escape
Your freedom, your chance

I was forewarned and eager
I would witness you emerge
Words were clear, Doc said
We will come back and get you
It never happened.

My instincts informed me
You were making trouble, like me
Just like me
I didn't know if the world was ready,
But I was.

I raced out of the waiting room
I needed to stand my post
Under all the lights, like on TV
Right by the bedside
To hear your first cry,
My first

But there you were:
Out of the womb, rolling,
Being pushed down the hall
I was too happy; I knew,
I just knew you were all me.

THERAPY

It's hard to imagine that I would be sitting here spilling my guts to you, letting you in on my deepest thoughts. I feel you are the only one I can talk to, the only one who absorbs everything I say word for word, emotion for emotion. What makes it easy is the way you read between the lines and never skip ahead. Your patients even reflect your listening skills, and the way you never move unless I move you gives me the feeling that I have full control of this session.

I have been humbled by my past experiences, yet they haunt me like a demon in the night. I know that without them, I wouldn't be the person I am today, so I wouldn't go back to change anything. But damn that violence that I witnessed and experienced growing up... What were they thinking? What were we thinking? What was I thinking? I guess I'll never know...

These moments replay in my mind, and I think about how I would react to these events differently. I eventually snap back into reality, but damn those moments hurt. My time is about to be up, so I will continue with you next time. I have more to tell you...

THERAPY II: ME AND MY POPS

My father was an alcoholic;
I didn't know much about him.
I know he liked to smoke cigarettes
and listen to soulful 70s music.

I never knew how he treated his family.
All I know is that he worked
and lived in the same place forever.
Therefore, I can say he was a provider.

I was never mad, just disappointed.
Like waking up on Christmas and the
thing you wanted most was not under the tree.
I was born and raised in Brooklyn,
but he never came to visit me in New York.
Every time I came to Virginia to visit,
my grandmother would force me to call him.
"Go see your father," she would tell me.

I was always uncomfortable around him.
Perhaps it was because I didn't know him...
When I was an adult, I moved to Virginia
and reached out to him.
We had a good relationship:
He called me regularly, and I visited often.
I often stopped by and would take my kids to see him.

I remember him tossing a football to my son.
I remember him holding my daughter.

Our relationship sprouted as we drew close,
so I took it hard when he died!

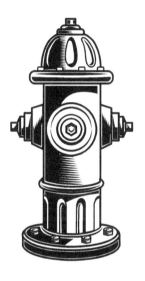

SECTION 6

EMPOWERMENT & SOLIDARITY

BLACK QUEENS

Black Women mean the world:
tilted with distress, rotating continuously.
She is a product of her environment:
drugs, alcohol, poverty, coated segregation.
Yet, she never loses her beauty, her worth.
Everything to her children came blessed:
the earth, water, air... all priceless.
That's why you remain Black Queens!

HIP HOP SOUND

At recess, the kids played in a yard,
separated like a gated community from the outsiders—
a separation well-needed to keep non-attending kids out.
There was hop-Scotch, double Dutch,
tag, football, handball, and flies-up.

The outsiders with their baggy jeans,
hats to the back, cool-swaggered, looked in on the fun
with little-to-no regard—their eyes seemingly aware of where they,
the cutters, dropouts, and misfits needed to be: in the gate.

Suddenly, there was a bass sound that would make grandma quiver
and captured the attention of both the insiders and those out:
Do The Humpty Hump... Do The Humpty Hump!
The bass ran through their little bodies like a glass of water
at midnight, shaking the concrete and bouncing off
the school's brick structure, giving the youth a double dose.
They were all mesmerized: *Do The Humpty Hump... Do The Humpty Hump!*
Racing to the gate to get a closer look at where this amazing
sound was coming from, handballs, footballs, and jump-ropes
all dropped, and bodies started to rock—the girl's hips rotating
and the boy's heads bobbing. The bass and the words
kept hypnotizing them: *Do The Humpty Hump... Do The Humpty Hump!*

The outsiders surrounded the guilty truck like it was selling
ice cream on a hot summer day. They felt the music
whereas the insiders with their belts tight, pants creased,
and well-groomed presence looked out with little-to-no regard.
In a change of event, eyes were seemingly aware of where
they needed to be: outside of the gate, *Doing The Humpty Hump*

THE BALL PARK

I wake on a beautiful morning where the birds sing a delightful song, and I look out the window up to the sky, watching the clouds race across its blue surroundings. A smile ascends upon my face, knowing this will be a great summer day.

I reach for my shorts and slide them on. With highlights flashing through my mind providing the necessary confidence needed to compete with these Brooklyn ballers, I make my way downstairs and head to the courts.

Opening the front door, the clouds are no more. My smile leaves as I walk past the overflowing garbage cans, stepping on to the streets and being approached by begging hands wanting coins. I have no change to give, so hands turn down. Stray cats scuttle back and forth while life's addictions show face on both the dealer and user.

My mood changes as my face turns sour. Life's bittersweet taste since witnessing reality makes my face age twenty years within twenty seconds. Wrinkles make the world cautious and permit me to crease through everything and everyone on my way to the ball court.

My demeanor holds constant, but my destination is known to make personal struggles vanish temporarily. Echoes ring as hands clap boards. Moves made and cheers pave the way for excitement and glory, so I pick up the pace using a slight jog to keep my cool, yet my heart holds true because what lies ahead is heaven. I arrive, and I am greeted with hugs and pounds from competition throughout the neighborhood. Laughter and comedic insults are as normal as the air we breathe, thus no one takes offense on the ball court, where there is a common goal that everyone is shooting for.

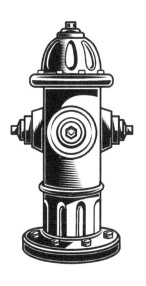

SECTION 7

REFLECTIONS ON CULTURE

PREDISPOSITION

My Father was an Alcoholic,
His Father was an Alcoholic,
My Uncle and His Brother were Alcoholics...

My Uncle and Aunt were Crackheads,
My Other Uncle was a Dope Fiend,
His Brother was a Dope Fiend and Crackhead.

My Mother was a Pothead,
Her Sister was a Pothead,
Their Aunts were Potheads.

My Stepfather was an Alcoholic and Pot Head,
My Other Stepfather was the Substance Dealer.
I lived in the Dope Spot.

I tried to hide the weed from My Aunt.
When she smelled it on me, she said,
"About Damn Time."

How the hell am I supposed to turn out?

FORGIVE THE ENVIRONMENT

You ran wild in your teens; it's funny how the streets pulled you in.
Alcohol and drugs turned you loose; your swagger and lingo adapted.
You swayed away from your home, your training, your daddy's words:
Cutting class, smoking weed, drinking brews, carrying knives and guns...
Doing things that boxed you in, sought respect from peers, and earned it.
Coming from a loving family, that wasn't your path,
but you were the first one to come back to reality because of love.
They say home is where the heart is, so you couldn't get too far.

The streets may have had you for a while, but love had you for life.
You realized that the streets were a trap and sought out God for guidance.
Boy, he didn't let you down. It's impressive how you gathered strength...
Who could blame you? You grew up running around with boys from your block:
dusty feet, throwing stones, most of the time just having fun,
laughing, spending nights playing tag and cracking jokes.
Then, shootings, stabbings, slashings, beatings, experienced or witnessed,
take control of the thoughts. The fun fades while dramatics endure!

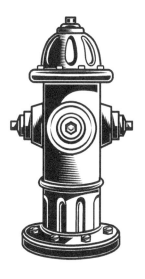

SECTION 8
MISC.

HANNIBAL'S WAR

He was a brilliant military mind,
strategist, and tactical genius
who was destined for war with the greatest
on an unimaginably successful expedition.
He was born to administer war
as the son of Carthaginian general
and was made to never befriend the enemy.

With knowledge of takings to conquest
and placement of a country upon his back,
he was young and in command.
A deadly combination well-authorized,
war was historically his by nature.

In his eastward stomping grounds,
he left a trail of chaos behind him.
Elements added danger,
but his march was not undone.
Elephants in this circus, unstoppable,
crippling the empire.

Rerouted Roman alliance!
His unclear, purposeful success became cloudy.
Stronghold sturdy, yet what was next?
Complexions ideological, defensive.
Residence left insecure
and fate lay back home,
allowing the powerful
to rule continuously.

AUTHOR'S BIO

Terrell L. Cuffee is an emerging writer whose storytelling invites his readers to introspect and get to know themselves on a soul level. Hailing from Brooklyn, he has been well-acquainted with the written word for over two decades. He may have not shared his words with the world at first, but the art of poetry and other forms of creative writing has always served as his ultimate therapy and sanctuary, where he freely expresses his heart's innermost stirrings. When he isn't immersed in creative pursuits, you can find this ambitious writer playing sports, spending quality time with his kids, binge-watching TV shows, or relaxing at the beach. Terrell has also been a coach for Youth Football and works in the Behavioral Health field.

Printed in the USA
CPSIA information can be obtained
at www.ICGtesting.com
JSHW021925200923
48799JS00001B/70